101 SPORTS JOKES

101 SPORTS JOKES

by Sam Schultz / pictures by Joan Hanson

guaranteed to
make you
a winner

Creative Paperbacks, Inc.
North Mankato, MN 56001

Published by Creative Paperbacks, Inc., North Mankato, Minnesota 56001.

Copyright © 1982 by Lerner Publications Company

All rights reserved. International copyright secured.
No part of this book may be reproduced in any form whatsoever
without permission in writing from the publisher except for
the inclusion of brief quotations in an acknowledged review.

Library of Congress Cataloging in Publication Data

Schultz, Sam.
  101 sports jokes.

  (Make me laugh!)
  Summary: A collection of 101 jokes and riddles about
such sports as football, baseball, basketball, soccer,
fishing, and hunting.
  1. Sports—Anecdotes, facetiae, satire, etc.
2. Wit and humor, Juvenile. [1. Sports—Wit and humor.
2. Jokes. 3. Riddles] I. Hanson, Joan, ill.
II. Title. III. Title: One hundred one sports jokes.
IV. Title: One hundred and one sports jokes. V. Series:
Make me laugh! (Mankato, Minn.)
PN6231.S65S3 1982b   818'.5402   82-18349
ISBN 0-89812-293-7 (pbk.)

Benny: My mother told me I'm not to play
football with my glasses.
Jenny: You won't have to. We're playing with a
football.

Q: Why does it take longer to run from second base to third base than from first base to second base?

A: Because there's a shortstop between second and third.

Joey gave his baseball coach a jar full of flies.

Coach: What's this for?

Joey: You told me to go home and practice catching flies. Here's a jar full. I caught every one of them!

Q: What kind of dog is a fighter?

A: A Boxer.

Johnny: Mom, I'm going out to play football.

Mom: With your brand new shirt?

Johnny: No, with the kids next door!

Q: Why don't chickens make good baseball players?
A: They can only hit fowl balls.

Bert: Did you ever see a catfish?
Gert: Don't kid me. Cats don't fish.

Brother: Hey, Sis, did I tell you about the touchdown I made?
Sister: No, and I appreciate it!

Jimmy: Mom, will you please give me a dollar for a man who's crying in the ballpark?
Mom: What's he crying about?
Jimmy: He's crying, "Hot dogs, one dollar!"

Fisherman: Tell me, what do you do when you get a bite?
Girl: Scratch it.

Mother: Nancy, why don't you play tennis with Freddy anymore?
Nancy: Would you play with someone who keeps lying about the score?
Mother: Certainly not!
Nancy: Neither would Freddy!

John: I always wear two pairs of pants when
   I go golfing.
Ron: Why?
John: In case I get a hole in one!

Q: Why is it always cool in a football stadium?
A: Because it's full of fans.

Q: Why is bowling called a quiet sport?
A: Because you can always hear a pin drop.

Mom: What are you doing home, Willie?
   I thought you were at baseball practice.
Willie: I was. But I hit the ball over the fence and
   the manager told me to run home!

Q: Who can go as fast as a race horse?
A: The jockey.

Joey: I made a 90-yard run in football today.
Tom: Hey, that's wonderful, Joey!
Joey: Not so wonderful. I couldn't catch the guy
  in front of me who had the ball.

Jimmy: My mother got a medal for racing.
Timmy: What kind of racing?
Jimmy: Raising a family!

Uncle: What do you want to be when you grow up, Junior?

Junior: I want to be a tough charging lineman on a football team.

Uncle: Well, you can be sure I won't stand in your way!

Carol: Did you enjoy the baseball game?

Barb: No, it reminded me of bad pancakes. Neither team had a good batter.

Owner of Lake: Young man, there's no fishing here!

Boy Fishing: You're telling me! I've been fishing here for two hours, and I haven't had a bite yet.

Mother: Time to get up, Joe. It's five to eight.

Joe: Who's winning?

Freddie: I ran 95 yards for a touchdown, and they kicked me off the team.
Larry: Why did they do that?
Freddie: Because I ran the wrong way!

Teacher: Class, who knows who defeated the Philistines?
Student: I think it was the New York Yankees.

Leslie: Dad, remember how you always used to worry that I'd break a window when I played baseball in the back yard?
Dad: Yes, I remember.
Leslie: Well, you can stop worrying now!

Dentist: Where do your teeth ache?
Child: First row—right field.

Jean: I don't play tennis because it's too noisy.
Joan: Noisy?
Jean: Yeah, everybody raises a racket.

First Hunter: I just ran into a big bear!
Second Hunter: Did you let him have both
   barrels?
First Hunter: Heck, I let him have the whole gun!

Quarterback: Are you hurt?
Halfback: I think so. Better call me a doctor.
Quarterback: Okay. You're a doctor.

Jane: Mom, we played baseball today and I stole
second base!
Mom: Well you march right back to school and
give it back!

Fred: How's the fishing around here?
Ned: It's okay.
Fred: Then how come you haven't caught any
fish?
Ned: You asked me about fishing, not catching.

Billie: My mother went horseback riding and got
a headache.
Millie: That's not where *I* ache when I go
horseback riding!

Son: Dad, you should have seen the baseball game I saw today. The bases were loaded, the batter made a home run, and not a man scored.
Dad: How come?
Son: It was a girls' baseball team!

Gym Teacher to Boxer: Stay down till nine!
Boxer: I can't! I've got another class at 8:30!

Q: What can you serve but not eat?
A: A tennis ball.

Baseball Player: Son, would you please get my fielder's glove out of the car?
Son (Later): Dad, I can't find it!
Player: Where did you look?
Son: In the glove compartment!

Q: Why is a football called a pigskin?
A: Because most football players like to "hog" the ball.

Coach: What's the best way to hold a bat?
Player: By the wings!

Sarah: Hey, Pat, why aren't you wearing your baseball uniform?

Pat: Because my doctor said I can't play baseball.

Sarah: Heck, I could have told you that a long time ago!

Safari Leader: If you see a leopard, shoot him on the spot.

Hunter: There's a leopard. Quick, which spot?

Little Boy: How many fish have you caught, Mister?

Fisherman: None yet, but I've only been fishing for an hour.

Little Boy: That's better than the man who was fishing here yesterday.

Fisherman: How is it better?

Little Boy: It took him five hours to do what you've done in just one!

Linda: Want to come watch our game? We're the
  champions so far.
Katie: Are you really?
Linda: Sure, it's our first game of the season!

Rookie Player: What does it take to hit a ball the
  way you do?
Veteran Ball Player: A bat.

Q: What did the bucking bronco say to his rider
  at the rodeo?
A: "Get off my back!"

Julie: My father went hunting, and he shot three
  ducks.
Sam: Were they wild?
Julie: No, but the farmer who owned them was.

Tom: Look what I caught! A jellyfish!
Ron: Really? What flavor?

Eddie: Mommy, I just found a lost football.
Mommy: How do you know it's lost?
Eddie: Because the kids down the street are still
   looking for it!

Dick: According to my watch, I can run 100
    yards in 10 seconds.
Rick: My watch runs slow, too.

Louie: I came home early from baseball practice
    because I didn't want to get sick.
Mother: What do you mean?
Louie: I told the coach I wanted to be the
    catcher, and he told me the only thing I'll ever
    catch is a cold!

Cathy: How do you make a fisherman's net?
Patsy: Just sew a lot of holes together!

Coach: Why do you think you'll make a good
    football player?
Student: Because I've got athlete's feet!

Umpire: I have to admit, the kids on your team are good losers.
Coach: Good? They're perfect!

Mary: Look at the fish I caught!
Larry: Wow! That's a big one. What are you going to do with it?
Mary: I'm going to take it home for dinner.
Fish: No thanks. I already had dinner!

Swimmer: Are there any alligators in this swamp?
Swamp Dweller: I don't think so. The sharks scare them away!

Child (At first baseball game): Dad, why is that man running?
Father: Because he hit the ball.
Child: Is he afraid he's going to get spanked?

Boy: What kind of fish is that?
Fisherman: Smelt.
Boy: Sure does. But what kind of fish is it?

Ralph: Do you know what Lisa did after she won
the swimming meet?
Jimmy: No, what did she do?
Ralph: She dried herself off!

Georgie: I was down at the lake and I saw a
   catfish.
Porgie: Did it catch anything?

Jerry: My brother makes about 15 baskets a day.
Ginny: Is he a basket weaver?
Jerry: No, he's a basketball player!

First Camper: Did you clean that fish before you
   put it into the fry pan?
Second Camper: What for? I just pulled it out of
   the water.

Mother: Why are you home so early from
   practice?
Susie: I just got bored playing left.
Mother: Left field?
Susie: No, left out.

First Little League Manager: Your team made
more errors than any team I've ever seen!
You should have left half your team home.
Second Manager: I did.

Billy: Boy, am I glad I'm not a fish.
Willy: Why?
Billy: Because they spend all their time in
schools!

Q: Where is the biggest diamond in the world?
A: Yankee Stadium.

Barney: I'm taking a course in parachute
jumping.
Arnie: How many jumps do you have to make
before you pass the course?
Barney: All of them!

Mother: Billy, I don't want you to play with anyone who cheats or steals.

Billy: Does that mean I can't play with Henry next door?

Mother: Why not? Does he cheat?

Billy: No, but we played baseball yesterday, and he stole second base!

Ross: I went crab fishing, and a crab bit off one of my toes.

Ann: Which one?

Ross: How should I know? All crabs look alike.

Son: Dad, I've been dreaming about baseball
every night for a week!
Dad: Why don't you try dreaming about
something else?
Son: What? And miss my turn at bat?

Q: What has 18 legs and flies?
A: A baseball team.

Ronnie: Shh! I'm hunting for lions!
Donnie: There are no lions here.
Ronnie: If there were, I wouldn't have to hunt for
them.

Mike: I can't go swimming right now. I just ate,
and my mother said I shouldn't swim on a full
stomach.
Rosie: Then swim on your back!

Mike: I had to quit the basketball team because the coach got sick.

Ike: What has that to do with your quitting the team?

Mike: He got sick of watching me play.

Q: What did one fish say to another fish after it was hooked?

A: "That's what you get for not keeping your mouth shut."

Q: What did the ball player get for hitting the ball out of the park?

A: A home run.

Bobby: I fell down a dozen times while ice skating today.

Jeff: Did anyone make any funny cracks?

Bobby: Only the ice.

Dennis: Timmy isn't our quarterback anymore because of his mother.

Harvey: Why? What did she do?

Dennis: She told him not to pass anything until somebody said, "Please."

Ann: Sally, how come you're catching so many
fish and I'm not catching any?
Sally: I don't know. I guess your worm just isn't
trying hard enough.

Baseball Manager to Outfielder: You've been missing a lot of balls out there. If you can't do any better, I'm going to have to put another player in the outfield!

Outfielder: Gee, thanks! I sure could use some extra help.

Penny: I just saw a man-eating shark!

Denny: Where?

Penny: In the restaurant at the end of the pier!

Q: A girl was hit in the head at a baseball game. Guess what came out of her mouth?

A: A bawl.

Q: What do eggs and a losing ball team have in common?

A: They both get beaten.

Helen: I bet I can tell you the score of this soccer game before it starts.
Ellen: Okay, smartie, tell me.
Helen: Nothing to nothing.

Umpire: Hey, kid, that was only strike two. You have another one coming.
Batter: I don't want it!

Arnie (Pulling fish out of water): This fish sure must be happy to be caught!
Barnie: What makes you think so?
Arnie: Look how it's wagging its tail.

Sherry: What's the difference between a strike and a ball?
Jerry: I don't know.
Sherry: Okay, then you can be umpire for our game.

Artie: Why do you keep falling down? Can't you ice skate?

Marty: I'm not sure. I've never been on my feet long enough to find out!

Some neighborhood kids were playing football.
Little Leo kept fumbling the ball.
Paul: That Leo is terrible! Why do we let him
play on our team?
Saul: We've got to. It's his ball!

Two kids were fishing. A younger kid came by
  and watched them.
Younger Kid: What are you guys doing? Fishing?
Older Kid: No, we're drowning worms.

Judy: My dad just came back from hunting man-
  eating tigers.
Trudy: Did he have any luck?
Judy: He sure did. He never came across any!

Steve: This lake must be full of trout.
Rob: What makes you think so?
Steve: We haven't caught any!

Hunter: Say, have you seen a deer around here?
Farmer: Yes.
Hunter: How long ago?
Farmer: About a year.

Man in Fish Market: Throw me a fish!
Fish Market Clerk: What for?
Man: So I can show my family the fish I caught!

Jerry: My dad went hunting with our neighbor
    and he shot this stuffed tiger.
Terry: What's it stuffed with?
Jerry: Our neighbor.

Game Warden: You kids can't fish without a
    permit!
Chris: Not so. We're using worms, and the fish
    are biting like crazy!

Betty fell into the lake while fishing. A man passed
    by and helped her out of the water.
Man: How'd you come to fall in?
Betty: I didn't. I came to fish.

Jan: Why are you swimming with your coat on?
Ann: Because the water's cold!

Q: What do a bat and a fly swatter have in common?

A: They both hit flies.

Q: What did one football say to another
football?
A: "People get a kick out of me!"

Old Man: Did you ever take home a fish this size,
sonny?
Sonny: No, sir. I always throw the little ones
back.

The big kids were playing the little kids in
football. One of the little kids dropped the ball.
He called to Sally to pick it up. "No way!" said
Sally. "*I* didn't drop it!

Q: Why didn't a single man get a hit at a baseball
game?
A: Because only married men played!

ABOUT THE AUTHOR

SAM SCHULTZ began telling jokes to children when his own were very young, and today he likes to think up new jokes while jogging on the beach near his home in Santa Monica, California. Mr. Schultz has been a writer for several advertising agencies, and now he writes scripts for television shows and children's films.

ABOUT THE ARTIST

JOAN HANSON lives with her husband and two sons in Afton, Minnesota, a tiny village on the St. Croix River. Her distinctive, deliberately whimsical pen-and-ink drawings have illustrated 30 children's books. Ms. Hanson is also an accomplished weaver, and while that art form takes up most of her time, she enjoys sketching and finds it a refreshing change from her weaving.

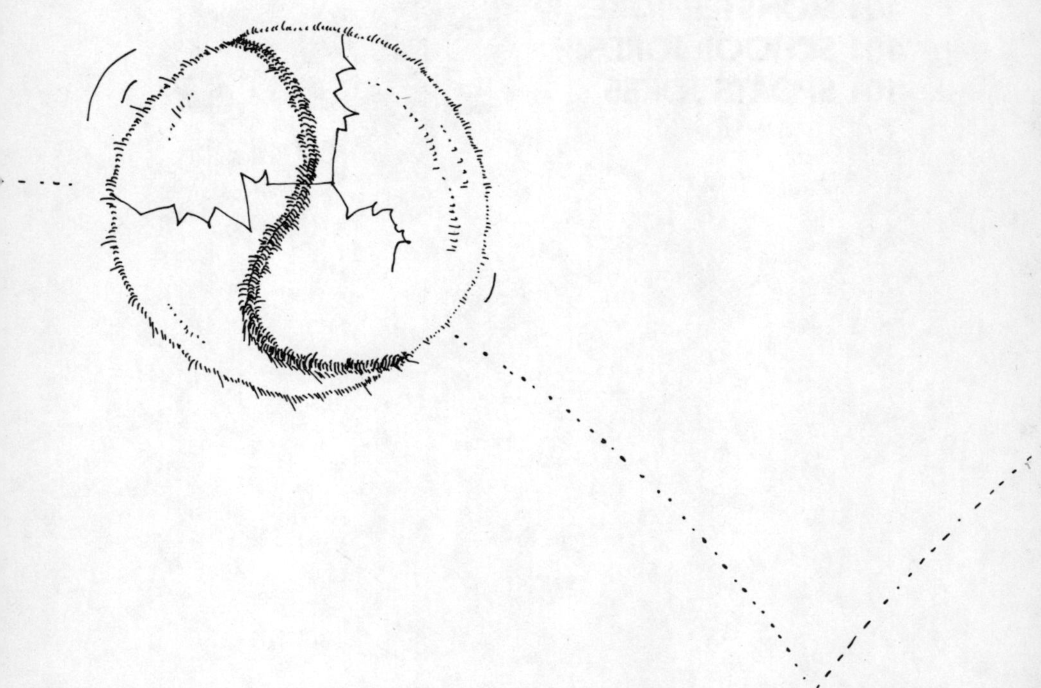

Make Me Laugh!

101 ANIMAL JOKES
101 FAMILY JOKES
101 KNOCK-KNOCK JOKES
101 MONSTER JOKES
101 SCHOOL JOKES
101 SPORTS JOKES

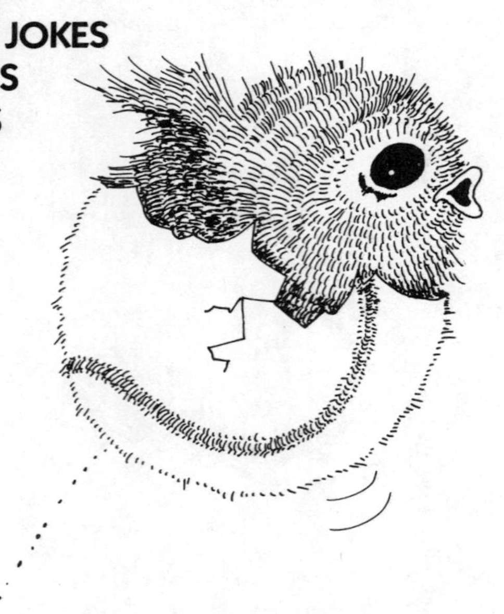